Boiling a Frog

Christopher was born in Glasgow in 1967 and has been working as a playwright since the mid-1990's. He has worked with 7:84, Complete Productions, Borderline, and his own theatre company, mct, with plays such as *Free-Fall* (shortlisted for Soho Theatre's Verity Bargate Award 2004), *Boiling a Frog* (adapted from the novel by Christopher Brookmyre), *It is Done*, *Cut to the Chase*, *Another Space*, *Molly's Collar and Tie* and *Smells and Bells*. He was Playwriting Fellow at the Traverse Theatre during 2005 and Associate Playwright at Playwrights' Studio Scotland in 2006. He has also written for radio, television, various pantomimes and cabaret revues. His work as a dramaturg, teacher and script/workshop facilitator is extensive, working with the Citizens' Theatre, National Theatre of Scotland, Glasgay!, The Traverse's Class Act project, Glasgow University, Coatbridge College and many others. He is a former Chair of the Scottish Society of Playwrights.

fairplay press

Boiling a Frog

by Christopher Deans

Adapted from the novel by Christopher Brookmyre

fairplay press

First published by fairplay press, an imprint of Capercaillie Books Limited in 2008.

Registered office 1 Rutland Court, Edinburgh.

© Christopher Deans and Pergopolynices Ltd. 2008. The moral right of the author has been asserted.

Printed in the UK.

A catalogue record for this book is available from the British Library.

ISBN 978-1-906220-14-3

The publisher acknowledges support from the Scottish Arts Council towards the publication of this title.

 Scottish **Arts** Council

With thanks to Lorenzo

Characters

JUDGE

JACK PARLABANE

FOOALTIYEMAN

ELSPETH DOYLE

IAN BEADIE

TEDDY GRAHAM

PETER LOGAN

PAULA REID

MIKE BRIGGS

SARAH

CARDINAL DOOLLAN

FATHER FRANCIS SHELLEY

ROSS QUINN

CHRISTIE

DAVID SANDERSON

WAITRESS/WAITER

PHOTOGRAPHER

SALES REP

TECHNICIAN

GUARDS

POLICE OFFICERS

Production Note

First produced at Paisley Arts Centre on 3rd February 2005 with the following cast and production team:

KATE DICKIE: Fooaltiyeman, Sarah and Waiter

ROBBIE JACK: Peter Logan, Cardinal Doollan, Ross Quinn, David Sanderson, Photographer, Sales Rep and Technician

GARY McINNES: Jack Parlabane

LINDA McLAUGHLIN: Elspeth Doyle, Christie and Guard 2

STEWART PORTER: Ian Beadie

ROSS STENHOUSE: Judge, Teddy Graham, Mike Briggs, Father Shelley, Kevin and Guard 1

DIRECTOR: Lorenzo Mele

ASSISTANT DIRECTOR: Brenda Murphy

COMPOSER: Robert Burlin

SET DESIGNER: Becky Minto

Prologue

PARLABANE hovers inside the Catholic Headquarters – clasping a file in his hands. He is about to get away.

PARLABANE: Gotcha! Amphibians are poikilothermic; their body temperatures adapt automatically to changes in their environment, without their noticing. Theoretically, this means that if you were to put a frog in a pan of cold water, then turn up the heat gradually, you could cook the poor creature to death before it even realised it was in danger.

PARLABANE is about to make his escape when flashlights dazzle him, and he is blinded to the spot, gazing helplessly at the police who have captured him.

Act 1

Scene 1

PARLABANE stands before a judge in a courtroom.

JUDGE: John Lapsley Parlabane – that you stand before this court today comes as no great surprise. For a tiresome number of years now, you've thrust your ill-informed, half-baked, and frankly, paranoid theories into the faces of Scotland's great and august institutions. Where you've not found wrongdoings you've imagined – or worse – implied them.

You now stand here before me – having this time pitted yourself against the Catholic Church – and bitten off more than you can chew.

This is a new Scotland, a new country, with new standards and a new morality. I can see no future for your likes here and I must not allow it or its institutions – nascent and ancient alike – to be disparaged and prejudiced by the diseased mind of a wee shite like you. For this reason, I order that you be taken from this court, henceforth to a place of confinement, there to dwell in perpetual fear of being chibbed and humped by rabid schemies. Take him down.

Scene 2

PARLABANE stands in his cell – the door is closed behind him.

PARLABANE: Go on, do your worst. See if I care. You think I'm scared of pain and misery? Let me tell you about pain and misery, pal.

PARLABANE goes to sit down on bed. As he does he sits on FOOALTIYEMAN, his emaciated cell-mate. He recoils and bumps head on the upper bunk.

FOOALTIYEMAN: Ah-hahahahahaha – fuckin' waaank! Fuckin' daft cunt ya.

PARLABANE: **(PARLABANE will act as narrator throughout the play and will address the audience at specific moments.)** Who in God's name was this sneering anorexic gargoyle?

FOOALTIYEMAN laughs.

PARLABANE: Let me tell you, if this guy had been in Belsen, his nickname would have been Slim.

FOOALTIYEMAN: Fooaltiyeman, that looked fuckin' sair. Hahaha-hahaha. Serve ye fuckin' right, sittin' there when it's ma fuckin' bed.

PARLABANE: I'll take the top one, shall I?

FOOALTIYEMAN: Fuckin' first time, innit, eh? Fuckin' shitin' it I bet. Fooaltiyeman, I don't like the look o' your chances, ne'er I don't. Fuckin' seen it aw afore, man, fuckin' awyit, an' fuckin' . . . fuckin' cunts like you cannae hack it. Fuckin' twirly sheets job man, altiye. Fuckin' waaank.

PARLABANE: I can honestly say – in all my years mixing with the good the bad and the downright ugly of Scottish life – this was the least charming of the whole sorry bunch. And when I tell you I'm a journalist, and through my wife's job I've met a fair few surgeons, that takes some beating.

Silence.

FOOALTIYEMAN: Don't take the huff. Just kiddin ye oan like, n'at, know? Just a wee joke, man. I mean yir heid – is it ok? It looked fu . . . **(Stops.)** . . . sair fae here.

PARLABANE: He wanted something. His bulging desperate eyes were staring at me like Bambi's mother just before the slaughter. He didnae even need to ask. Look mate, I've no cigarettes.

FOOALTIYEMAN: Fuckin' come oan. Just gie's a fag. Just wan.

PARLABANE: I don't smoke. Sorry.

FOOALTIYEMAN: Fuckin' stop an' search time then, innit? An' altiye, if I fuckin' fin any fags, you're getting' a fuckin' skelp, man. Alfuckintiye.

FOOALTIYEMAN searches PARLABANE.

PARLABANE: It reminded me of that joke about a new arrival in hell. The bloke gets shown a door and told – *you're in there* – by his accompanying imp. Once inside, he finds a bunch of men sitting up to their necks in shit, drinking cups of tea. This isn't so bad he says to himself. Get used to the smell and it might even seem quite civilised. At which point another imp sticks his head round the door and says, right lads, tea-break's over. Back on your heids.

FOOALTIYEMAN lets out a sound of glee. He's seen something on the floor – a used tea-bag.

FOOALTIYEMAN: Ya dancer.

PARLABANE: A used tea-bag?

FOOALTIYEMAN: Like gold dust roon here man.

FOOALTIYEMAN proceeds to roll-up tea-bag whilst PARLABANE speaks.

PARLABANE: It was true then – I *was* the one and only sane Scottish bloke in a world gone off its – excuse the French – fuckin' heid. Then again, having done what I'd just done, that well-worn phrase – only yirself tae blame – was pure stickin tae the back ae my throat.

Scene 3

A restaurant. Several months previously. ELSPETH DOYLE and IAN BEADIE are having dinner.

BEADIE: You? Bitter? Elspeth Doyle? Naw.

ELSPETH: Of course I'm bloody bitter. I feel like Debbie Reynolds in *Singing in the* flipping *Rain*. It's my work behind the scenes that's keeping the show on the road, but its been made crystal clear they don't want me out in front of the audience.

BEADIE: Look – your glass is empty – let me top you up.

BEADIE tops her glass up. He doesn't top up his own.

PARLABANE: This one had put all her energy into making New Labour packaging as important as what's in the box, so why be surprised when they decide she wasn't saleable and sexy enough for the front benches?

ELSPETH: Called everything from a half-chewed toothbrush to wicked witch of the west. I've never had any bloody illusions about being a glamour-puss, but it's not even that that's the obstacle. It's not just me that's isn't sexy enough – it's my politics.

BEADIE: Aye, well I was gaunny say, look at Margaret Grier. She looks like she's no stranger tae a deep-fried Mars bar, but it hisane stopped her climbin' the greasy pole.

ELSPETH: Exactly. The problem with me is . . . all this is still off the record?

BEADIE: Oh come on, I'm no' a journalist any mair. Pat me down for Dictaphones – go on. Besides, why would I want to stitch you up? You're not important enough, remember? I mean, maybe if you hidnae been overlooked in the reshuffle . . .

ELSPETH throws her napkin at him.

ELSPETH: You're a bloody terror you.

Beat.

BEADIE: You know what Elspeth?

ELSPETH: Go on – tell me what I *should* be doing.

BEADIE: You're too good.

PARLABANE: What you after Beadie?

BEADIE: I've seen it happen time and time again – they simply don't want to move you because you're too useful where you are.

ELSPETH: Where am I? PR to what? I'm not exactly privy to the comings and goings of the New Labour elite.

Pause.

BEADIE: If I made you an offer, they'd promote you in a flash.

The thought of you dishing the dirt on that lot to a guy like me would fair grease the wheels.

ELSPETH: Uch Beadie – get away with you – you're drunk. We both are.

BEADIE: It's a sad day when they're sacrificing talents like yours on the altar of political correctness. You'll forgive the religious nature of my imagery – you being a diehard Tim and all. I think the party's so over-run with arse-bandits . . .

ELSPETH:Tut tut.

BEADIE: . . . these days, they wouldn't even notice that the Scottish public are a damn sight closer to your views.

ELSPETH: Maybe. But you – Iain Beadie – should choose your terms more diplomatically. We're living in more enlightened times.

BEADIE: Uch – you know what I mean. there's a lot of concerned voters out there. Me among them. I hate to think of my wee nephew Cameron havin' his heid filled wi' ideas he's no equipped tae handle, and startin' to think he's something he's no' just because he's confused.

ELSPETH: Maybe if I'd had kids myself. Maybe then I'd come across as a concerned mother.

Beat

BEADIE: But tell me Elspeth – you ever thought it's not just a snub?

ELSPETH: What?

BEADIE: Ever thought it's something mair?

ELSPETH: They've something bigger in mind for me? Don't make me laugh.

BEADIE: Mibbe the reason they didnae promote you wasn't necessarily about slapping you on the wrist. It could have been about keeping you out the picture. Mibbe they've got some new-fangled policies up their sleeve that they widane want the likes of you meddling with. Ever thought about that?

ELSPETH: No comment Mr Beadie

BEADIE: You're slippin' Elspeth. You could have just said no. No comment means there's something to comment on.

ELSPETH's pager beeps.

ELSPETH: Excuse me.

BEADIE: Her Master's Voice. **(Waits.)** What's it say?

Message: E.D. SOS . . . Got message from A.L. Peter Logan needs you on something urgently . . . Requested you by name . . . Go to 14 Royal Circus ASAP.

ELSPETH: **(distracted)** I'm needed. Here's my . . . **(Hands him money.)**

BEADIE: You look like you've just seen a ghost.

ELSPETH: **(referring to message)** I can't.

BEADIE: Waste ae my time, eh?

ELSPETH: **(referring to meal)** Thanks.

ELSPETH leaves.

Scene 4

ELSPETH enters, trips and falls flat on her face. She remains flat on the ground holding an inside-out umbrella aloft. The rain is very heavy.

PARLABANE: The party had feared that Elspeth Doyle had lurked around in the shadows so long she'd bumble around like a pit-pony if she ever emerged into the daylight.

ELSPETH: Bugger!

PARLABANE: So far – she wisnae letting them down.

ELSPETH picks herself up and wipes herself down.

ELSPETH: Bloody brollies!

She dumps the umbrella. She then rings the door-bell. TEDDY answers.

TEDDY: Hello?

ELSPETH: I'm here to see Peter.

PARLABANE: Peter Logan – MSP and glamour boy of New Labour.

TEDDY: **(suspiciously)** And who might you be?

ELSPETH: Elspeth Doyle. Sent by the party. This is the right house, isn't it? **(Points to nameplate.)** Logan? 14 Royal Circus?

TEDDY: Yes, it, I mean, maybe, I . . . who sent you?

ELSPETH: Who do you think?

TEDDY: It's just – they said you'd be a man.

ELSPETH: Sorry to disappoint. Look, can I come in?

TEDDY: And it's . . . Elspeth Doyle?

ELSPETH: Yes.

TEDDY: I'm sorry – I'm not very clued-up on these party things.

ELSPETH: Andrew Lawrie got John Cooper to page me. Said it was urgent. You haven't a clue what I'm talking about, do you?

TEDDY: Why don't you wait and talk to Peter.

ELSPETH: I would if I . . .

TEDDY: It's just, he's – erm – in the middle of something at the minute.

ELSPETH: So, you *are* a friend? Right?

TEDDY: Well . . . **(Hears noise in background.)** Ok – I suppose – but quickly – come in.

ELSPETH enters.

ELSPETH: Shall I . . . go in here?

TEDDY: Yes . . . that's . . . erm . . . a good idea. I'll go shout on him, shall I? **(Shouts.)** Peter!

ELSPETH steps inside – immediately impressed by its décor.

PARLABANE: Not a hint of Ikea about the place.

TEDDY speaks to PETER who is in other room.

TEDDY: Peter?

PETER: Yes?

TEDDY: The cavalry's arrived.

PETER: Oh thank Christ. Just a sec.

TEDDY: He's just . . .

PETER enters dressed in a bathrobe. As soon as he sees ELSPETH he lets out a scream.

PETER: Aaaaaaaghh!

TEDDY: Peter, what's wrong? Is it? . . .

PETER: What the hell is she doing here?

TEDDY: She's the cavalry, Peter. She was sent . . .

PETER: Elspeth bloody Doyle. Miss Puritan 1985. What the hell are you doing here?

ELSPETH: What do you mean? You asked for me. Personally. Via Andrew Lawrie. John Cooper . . .

PETER: John Coo . . . But . . . I didn't . . . I asked for Ewan Dickson. Why the hell would I? . . . Oh Jesus Christ. This isn't happening. Someone tell me this isn't happening. **(To TEDDY.)** Ewan Dickson. ED.

ELSPETH: Elspeth Doyle.

PARLABANE: ED. Whit a bloody fuck up. You'd think they'd come up with a better system.

PETER sits with head in hands. TEDDY looks confused. During the following ELSPETH can hear a faint buzzing sound that gets increasingly louder.

ELSPETH: Ewan Dickson's in London as far as I know.

TEDDY: **(ignoring ELSPETH)** Did you try that stuff?

PETER: Yes.

ELSPETH: Are you ill? I could phone a doctor.

TEDDY: I am a doctor. **(To PETER.)** You'll have to drink a lot of fluid.

PETER: This is a nightmare. All I need now is Michael Aspel to pop up with his big red book. Oh no – this isn't happening.

ELSPETH: Right. I don't see any further point in me being here. If it's alright with you gentlemen, I'm going to take my leave.

ELSPETH goes to door.

PETER: Stop!

TEDDY: Peter!

PETER: She's here now, isn't she? Who else I'm I going to get at this time? Elspeth – have a seat.

ELSPETH sits.

ELSPETH: Am I going mad or is something buzzing in here?

PETER: Christ. **(He moves – and the buzzing changes sounds.)**

ELSPETH: Hear it now?

TEDDY: I can't hear a thing.

ELSPETH: I'm sure I can hear something.

PARLABANE: Too right she could.

ELSPETH: Yes, it's definitely . . .

PETER: Elspeth my dear – it's a vibrator. And – without going into too many details – it's stuck up my ass.

ELSPETH: How the blazes?

PETER: I slipped getting out of the shower. Bloody stupid of me to leave a lubricated pocket-rocket standing upright on the bathroom floor, but I guess I'll never learn. Jesus Christ. How do you think?

TEDDY: Someone gave me it as a joke.

PETER: I think that's about as much as Elspeth would care to hear.

ELSPETH: And Ewan Dickson? He's got a big sink-plunger?

PETER: Oh, how very droll. How very.

The buzzing changes again.

ELSPETH: So, just to make sure I'm clear on the situation, because neither of us can afford mistaken assumptions Peter, you're telling me, is this right – that you're bisexual?

PETER: No.

ELSPETH: Just experimenting?

PETER: No.

ELSPETH: So what? Are we back to slipping coming out of the shower?

PETER:No. Though coming out might be an appropriate turn of phrase.

TEDDY: But coming out's not on the immediate agenda.

PETER: Too bloody right it isn't.

ELSPETH: So let me get this straight. **(Pause.)** You're gay?

PETER: Halle-bloody-lujah.

ELSPETH: Since when?

PETER: Since feeling up Marianne Clark at an under-fourteens disco, and realising it didn't exactly ring my bell.

ELSPETH: But, I mean – the party – who knows?

PETER: Who doesn't?

TEDDY: That's not quite true Peter. You're being melodramatic now.

PETER: A need-to-know basis. You know – the usual crap. It was felt I shouldn't go stoking the flames.

ELSPETH: It was felt?

PETER: Nothing's entirely your decision in politics.

ELSPETH: And all those models and TV stars you're seen with?

TEDDY: Keep drinking that water.

PETER: The tabloids just want the picture – me in a flash suit – some blond in a tight dress.

TEDDY: Preferably one where you can see her nipples.

ELSPETH: And you two?

PETER: Us two? Huh!

TEDDY: Ten years this June. Like an old married couple, aren't we?

ELSPETH: And you? Are you out?

TEDDY: You must be joking. Cardio-thorassic medicine? It's overrun with macho wankers.

PETER: I've principles. I campaigned against section 28. I did my bit. But remind me Elspeth – you supported it, didn't you?

ELSPETH: I've my principles too Peter.

PETER: Homophobic principles.

ELSPETH: The fact I supported it doesn't make me homophobic.

PETER: No Elspeth. Its your homophobia that makes you homophobic.

ELSPETH: I'm not ho . . .

PETER: Yes you are. And you're the worst kind – because you don't even realise the ways in which you are. The fully fledged gay-bashers are less bother.

TEDDY: I don't think this is the time to get all Peter Tatchell on us babes.

The buzzing gets very loud.

PETER: A doctor. I need a doctor

ELSPETH: But can't Teddy?

PETER: Preferably one that extracts dildos rather than shoves them up with gay abandon. Elspeth – help me. Please? Elspeth?

ELSPETH thinks.

ELSPETH: Ok Peter, I will. But I need to know – what will you do to help me?

Scene 5

ELSPETH and a pained-looking PETER LOGAN are entering the hospital. PAULA REID – looking harangued – stands to the side of them.

ELSPETH: Remember what I told you Paula – hold onto him.

PAULA: **(squeamishly touching him)** But it's not out yet.

PETER: She all you could get?

ELSPETH makes her grab hold of him.

ELSPETH: Any of the doctors ask – look at me – you're his girlfriend – right?

PAULA: I have done this before.

ELSPETH: You've been seeing him on and off for a few months – you were having a bit of fun – things just got out of hand – and you're to blame. Got it?

PAULA: And you're sure you can get me a weather slot on the telly?

ELSPETH: Yes!

Scene 6

Once more, PARLABANE stands in the middle of a cell.

BRIGGS: First time?

PARLABANE: Oh God – please spare me – not again.

BRIGGS: Mike Briggs, four years. Dope-smuggling.

PARLABANE: Jack Parlabane. Six months. B & E.

BRIGGS: Jakey sentence you got there.

PARLABANE: Can o' Fanta – as they say.

BRIGGS: You look like you're shitting yourself. Guards been windin' you up about me?

PARLABANE: Well . . .

While saying the following, BRIGGS is busy folding things away.

BRIGGS: You might think this place is full of nutters. And it is. Floor to ceiling. But that's like saying the arctic circle's full of snow. Same as the Eskimos, you need words to be able to distinguish between the different kinds of snow. And you'll need to be able to identify each kind of nutter round here so that you know who you're dealing with. If you think the bloke in front of you is a bam, but he turns out to be a nugget, for instance, then your tea could be well and truly out. You've also your zoomers, your screamers, your steamers and your rockets. Now don't ever fuck with a rocket.

BEADIE appears.

BRIGGS: A rocket is a steamer multiplied by a zoomer, to the power of a screamer. Total. Fucking. Nightmare. Malignant, petty, vengeful, sadistic and utterly unstable. But don't worry. You'll know one when you see one. They stand out a mile.

BEADIE receives a text.

BEADIE: Well, what do you know? Peter Logan – ya twisted wee pervert ye.

Scene 7

PARLABANE and SARAH at home.

PARLABANE: So, what was going on up at the hospital last night? All sounded a bit hush hush if you ask me.

SARAH: How did you? . . .

PARLABANE: Finger in every pie.

SARAH: Ah – but not this one you don't **(Realises she's let it slip.)** Shit!

PARLABANE: What? Something big?

SARAH: Just let it go.

PARLABANE: Sarah!

SARAH: You'll read about it soon enough.

PARLABANE: In that case, there's no harm giving me a sneak preview.

SARAH considers.

SARAH: No one – and I mean no one's to find out about this.

PARLABANE: Our dirty little secret. I like this.

SARAH: Promise me.

PARLABANE: Cross my heart and hope to die.

For some reason, she believes him.

SARAH: Ok. Guess who had a . . .

She considers how to phrase it.

SARAH: . . . vibrator extracted from their arse.

PARLABANE: Ugh! Sarah!

SARAH: Don't be such a prude. Your fingers have gone a wandering in that direction more than once.

PARLABANE: Heat of the moment love. **(Pause.)** Well – who was the lucky geezer? You've me all juiced up here.

SARAH: Peter Logan.

PARLABANE: Bloody hell.

SARAH: With that Catholic bigot Elspeth Doyle in tow – you know – her with the face like a hatchet.

PARLABANE: She wisnae the? . . .

SARAH: No, no – he'd some rent-a-bimbo from the telly, Paula Reid, draped all over him. And Jack – you are not breathing a word to a soul.

PARLABANE: Aye, right. This is ace.

SARAH: I mean it Jack.

PARLABANE: Sarah, I'm a bloody reporter.

SARAH: And I'm a doctor.

PARLABANE: Aye – but was he your patient?

SARAH: He was the hospital's. Uch, I knew I shouldn't have told you.

PARLABANE: But you did, didn't you?

SARAH: A moment of weakness. **(Beat.)** Anyway, you'd have found out eventually knowing you.

PARLABANE: Aye – because some other bugger's now got the story and will be coughing to the tabloids as we speak.

SARAH: Yes, and the informer won't be named – unlike the patient. Think about it. If you went with this story, I'd give it two, maybe three seconds before they cottoned on it was me who told you.

PARLABANE: Thinking like that doesn't really earn me my bread and butter petal.

SARAH: We can do without these particular crumbs. This isn't some Wee Free minister getting caught with his dick out. This is a . . .

PARLABANE: Self-absorbed arsehole who couldnae pass a mirror – or vibrator – as it turns out.

SARAH: So what? Peter Logan likes to put things up his bum. Where's the story in that? Eh? Gaunny tell me?

PARLABANE: An there ah was up for it tonight tae.

SARAH: What's next? Jack McConnell in diarrhoea shocker? Alex Salmond can't reach to wipe?

PARLABANE: Yip – that's definitely done it – no show tonight darling.

SARAH: That's why bedroom doors are closed. Sex is not a spectator sport.

PARLABANE: Oh, I don't know.

SARAH: And much as you may want to delude yourself about the quality of your performance wee man.

PARLABANE: Steady on!

SARAH: I don't think any of the expressions you make in the process are among those you'd pick for the cover of your autobiography.

PARLABANE: I was going to say that I once did this jobbie that . . .

SARAH whacks him.

PARLABANE: Ouch.

SARAH goes to leave.

SARAH: **(turning back to face him)** Who's he conning/betraying Jack? Who? And who's given you the right to stand there all high and mighty? Let he who is without sin cast the first stone. Isn't there going to be a time when we all grow up and act like adults?

PARLABANE: There something you and me should talk about here?

SARAH breaks down.

PARLABANE: **(perplexed)** Sarah?

SARAH rushes off. PARLABANE watches after her unable to work out what's just occurred.

That's one I didn't see coming.

Beat.

PARLABANE: But as I was to find out in the days, weeks and months ahead – in this world, sometimes there were a whole load more greater betrayals to be found than the ones in your own bedroom.

Act 2

Scene 1

CARDINAL DOOLLAN sits reading BEADIE's resume as FATHER SHELLEY looks on.

CARDINAL: It looks like you want to bring us down to operating at the level of our enemies, Father Shelley. See, I'm not sure this wouldn't be in itself a form of defeat.

SHELLEY: Your Eminence, the sad truth is that our enemies have already brought the battle down to that level, and it's a place where we are inexperienced and most vulnerable. Mr Beadie can show us how to fight there. I would urge you most sincerely to at least meet with the man and see what he has to say.

Pause.

CARDINAL: Very well, I'll grant him an audience.

SHELLEY: I mean, as you've read in his resume, he's fairly experienced in these matters.

CARDINAL: Who's his parish priest?

SHELLEY: I . . .

CARDINAL: Get me his priest on the phone and we'll chat.

SHELLEY: In a way, it is vital, even essential, that this man is not a Catholic, because his job would be to consider how our church looks from the outside, not from within.

CARDINAL: Then you are effectively entrusting the public image of the church in Scotland to someone who is not of the faith?

SHELLEY: Even if he bore us animosity – which I'm sure he doesn't – it would not be in the wider interests of his business to do anything less than his best job.

CARDINAL: Father Shelley, there have been many in the past who would sacrifice everything – their granny included – for an opportunity to do us ill.

SHELLEY: Mr Beadie's not interested in religion. What I mean is, I'm sure we can trust him. This is not unprecedented. Remember, back in the early nineties, there was a non-catholic editor of the *Celtic View*?

CARDINAL: Yes, I do remember hearing something about that. How did it happen again? Did he mislead them?

SHELLEY: No, Your Eminence, I think they merely forgot to ask. They just assumed. Turned out – there were no problems after all, and the young man did a fine job. He was, in a sense, entrusted with the public face of the football club, just as Mr Beadie would be of the church.

CARDINAL: And can you tell me how many trophies Celtic won while this young man was in charge of the club newspaper?

SHELLEY: He wasn't in charge of the team.

CARDINAL: How many, Father? **(Pause.)** Father Shelley, I'm waiting.

SHELLEY: None.

CARDINAL: None, Father Shelley.

SHELLEY: I'll phone Mr Beadie immediately and inform him we'll be choosing someone else.

CARDINAL: Perhaps Father Shelley, if you'd mentioned some of the non-Catholics who *were* in charge of the team. Jock Stein, for instance.

SHELLEY: I can assure you, your eminence, Mr Beadie is the Jock Stein of public relations.

Scene 2

BEADIE holds up a pamphlet to FATHER SHELLEY.

BEADIE: Tell me you didnae produce this? Just tell me ye didnae.

SHELLEY: Eh, no, I didn't as a matter of fact. However, this office is partly responsible for its distribution.

BEADIE: It's pure mince. I mean, what's it saying?

SHELLEY: Well, there is a certain amount of pressure brought by the NHS on Catholic doctors to carry out abortions.

BEADIE: Don't defend it. I understand why it's out there. But its tired. It's reductive. It makes you the victim. Pro-active, not reactive. You need to paint yourselves as a vibrant force within the country, in all walks of life. **(Beat.)** Tell me Father, exactly, how many Catholics are there in Scotland?

SHELLEY: Well, if you're talking bums on pews, then the figure alters radically depending on whether you're taking your snapshot on a wet Sunday in February or on Good Friday.

BEADIE: Father!

SHELLEY: On average, mass attendance is around 200,000, including kids. I mean, obviously there's a lot more nominal Catholics than . . .

BEADIE: Good. this is what I'm looking for. You mean baptised, catholic-educated, that sort of thing?

SHELLEY: Yes.

BEADIE: So how many of those?

SHELLEY: Ehm. I'd have to ask around, but I think its probably in the region of 700,000.

BEADIE: There you are. That's your figure. Well, actually, 700,000 – might as well say three quarters of a million. And if you're saying three quarters of a million, might as well round it up to 800,000. Eh?

SHELLEY: Well, I suppose so.

BEADIE: Don't suppose. It's now a fact. And it's a fact you have to reiterate as often as possible. When you refer to Cardinal Doollan, call him the leader of Scotland's 800,000 Catholics. Any time you talk to the press, get it in there, get it in there until it becomes like one word. Scotland's-eight-hundred-thousand-Catholics. Look at Bush. Fought an election on guns, God and gays. The corrupt wee shit managed four more years.

That's who you're representing Father – that's the mandate you have when you're dealing with the media. Not just 800,000 Catholics, but 800,000 Catholics with a political voice and a political will. A unified, dynamic, and motivated force of opinion.

PARLABANE: So it *was* true – religion is indeed a virus sent by some malevolent alien civilisation with an extremely busy colonisation programme. They know they're not going to get around to invading earth for a few thousand years, so in the meantime, they've decided – lets introduce religion, slow down the evolution process so that the buggers are still weak and primitive when we finally do turn up in the mothership.

(Pause.) But I suppose – looking back – it was statements like that from me that kind of hit a raw-nerve with some.

Scene 3

BEADIE's house in Eaglesham. BEADIE is seated round a table with FATHER SHELLEY and ELSPETH DOYLE.

BEADIE: What you are about to hear, you cannot take out of this room.

ELSPETH: Bit serious are you not Beadie?

BEADIE: Except in the case of Father Shelley to confide in Cardinal Doollan. If you so choose. This is information that's come from sources within the upper echelons of the Scottish executive, and not only must I protect my source, but we must protect Miss Doyle here.

ELSPETH: Sorry?

BEADIE: Whose religious beliefs would have her erroneously fingered for the leak if either of you were so rash as to open your big gubs.

ELSPETH: Beadie, what are you on about?

BEADIE: The information concerns what Labour party insiders are referring to as the Life Raft.

ELSPETH: How the hell did you? . . .

BEADIE: Trade secrets. I gave up trying to tap you for this sort of stuff a long time ago. So at least one of you know what I'm talking about. Should I go on?

ELSPETH: No – you bloody well won't.

SHELLEY: Well, since he's already begun.

ELSPETH: This is a scandal.

BEADIE: As is the Life Raft Elspeth. Now– hawd yir wheesht. The Life Raft – Father Shelley – is so called because it comprises a raft of proposed legislation – correct me if I'm wrong Elspeth – intended to breathe belated life into the Scottish parliament's flailing administration. Among the wide and varied Scandinavian inspired proposals – wait for this Father Shelley – you'll just love it – is the legal recognition of same-sex marriages within Scots law.

SHELLEY: In the holy name of God.

BEADIE: Exactly Father. **(Hands them files to read.)** Here – hiv a swatch. Now, don't be misled, this is not legislation quite yet.

ELSPETH: It's not even a formal proposal.

BEADIE: But I warn you Father, they're planning to test the water. New Labour are masters of making an idea seem palatable and even popular once they've decided it's winnable – and they think this one might be. Am I right Elspeth or am I not? Father, the bible may have taught you that there is a certain dignity about being the lone voice crying in the wilderness, but I'm sorry to inform you it disnae quite work that way in politics these days.

Scene 4

CARDINAL DOOLLAN's office. SHELLEY and the CARDINAL.

SHELLEY: It isn't the proposals themselves that present the gravest worry. It's the fact we are powerless to stop them.

CARDINAL: But we are not powerless to protest.

SHELLEY: But that would harm us more. That's Mr Beadie's whole point. We're being ignored – and the worst of it is that they can afford to ignore us – they know that. What we are looking at here is the end of the church as a serious political force.

CARDINAL: The voices of 800,000 Catholics can still make a powerful sound.

SHELLEY: If you can tell me where I might find 800,000 Catholics, I'll give it a go.

Beat.

CARDINAL: So, did anyone at this meeting have anything constructive to offer?

SHELLEY: Well, Mr Beadie spoke to me in private afterwards.

CARDINAL: And?

SHELLEY: Well, his proposal – it's perhaps not the most morally clear path.

Scene 5

BEADIE and ELSPETH are at the table in BEADIE's house later in the evening.

ELSPETH: What is it you're after Beadie?

BEADIE: It's not what I'm after Elspeth, it's what I can offer.

ELSPETH: That's you through and through – your generosity knows no bounds. You must think I'm some kind of halfwit.

BEADIE: Naw.

Beat.

ELSPETH: I'll tell you what I think, shall I?

BEADIE: Be my guest.

ELSPETH: I think you want me to stab my party in the back. You just haven't the guts to spell it out.

BEADIE: I want to help you.

ELSPETH: Shucks.

BEADIE: But only if you're prepared to help yourself.

ELSPETH: You mean only if I'm prepared to help you.

BEADIE: That would be a subsidiary benefit of this, aye, but you're the one who would stand to gain most.

ELSPETH: From stopping the Life Raft? Come off it. For one, it's still months away from going public. And by the time it does, I'd be surprised if there was one speck of anything contentious about it.

BEADIE: The time has never been better. Sex – drugs – religion:

three things everybody in politics is usually too wise or too cowardly to mess with. And not because of the public – but because of the press. And right now, the press is on the run, and the public have never had so small an appetite for prudish moralising. Your party knows fine well they can float this thing. They got away with an MSP having a dildo jammed up his bahookie for crying out loud. Is this the kind of party you want to be apart of?

ELSPETH: It's just struck me. You think I'm some miserable, homophobic old bat, don't you? What do I care if gays want to get married? I'm the one that's against promiscuity, remember? And as for cannabis – yeah – I care about that one. I'm bloody delighted about the idea of a Royal Commission because it would be proof that politicians act like adults. As a Catholic I'm not thrilled at the idea of Scottish Labour turning its back on its roots and abolishing denominational schools, but so what? That's a battle that hasn't even started, never mind finished, and I'd rather fight it from within the party, to make sure it does the right thing, thank you very much.

BEADIE: Then fight that battle and win it. Fight all your party battles and win them. That lot think the time is right for the Life Raft because the climate is right for a certain kind of idea and a certain kind of politician. But the climate can change. We can make it change.

ELSPETH: For Chrissake Beadie – you're no' in some James Bond film here.

BEADIE: What if the climate could be changed instantly? What if the political environment became censorious to the point of volatile? What if any whiff of sexual misconduct was career suicide and electoral poison? Wouldn't the Labour party want to heighten the profile of someone with a spotless reputation in that department – someone, in fact, who had already been identified in the public eye as a hammer of all things permissive and licentious?

ELSPETH: Aye – and suddenly I'd be the dog's bollocks. I get the picture. So – what would I need to do? Go down on Satan maybe? Or go down on you?

BEADIE: Well, you can do that if you like honey, but it wouldnae actually be necessary. One email. That's all you'd need tae send.

He holds up a disc.

SHELLEY: **(to CARDINAL)** One email.

ELSPETH: What's on it? And who'd I be sending it to? Oh, and why would I be sending it? Why not you?

BEADIE: Questions, questions.

ELSPETH: Well?

BEADIE: There's a wee file in this disc, disguised as a simple Word document, the content of which you can alter as appropriate so that it looks like a genuine memo. The chosen MSP double-clicks to read the file, and while he does, it discreetly installs a few wee nuggets.

He pauses to gauge her reaction.

BEADIE: They see your name as the sender, they'll be less inclined to subject it to security scans before opening.

ELSPETH: These wee nuggets?

Long silence.

ELSPETH: Well?

Pause.

BEADIE: Photographs of children.

ELSPETH: You whit?

BEADIE: Keep the heid.

ELSPETH: I'm out of here.

BEADIE: Hear me out. **(Grabbing hold of her.)** It's nothing too far out. In fact, the stuff's legal in most other countries. Naturist material – naked pictures of wee lassies on beaches or at campsites and what-have-you. But the point is – they're all under-age – fourteen, thirteen, maybe less.

ELSPETH: And you want me to? . . . You're away with the fairies.

BEADIE: I told you you'd go flying off. There's no way it can get back to you. The programme's fool-proof. They can say they knew nothing about the files, but their news browser will say something else. And these being private PC's no-one else had access to, they cannae claim a big boy done it and ran away. You getting the picture yet?

ELSPETH: You want me to frame my colleagues? Create a scandal that'll shatter our parliament and ruin my party? And this'll help me how?

BEADIE: We'll be throwing a Lib Dem and an SNP body on the pyre as well – wi' yir man Peter Logan on top of course. Eftir thon dildo shenanigans, the public will believe anything aboot him. Then it wont be a party issue – it'll be wan a morality. Sex will be the bogeyman of Scottish politics in no time. Within a week we'll be seein' the dawn of a new age of Puritanism – something we Scots have always been more comfortable with. And the churches are gaunny be brought right back into the game as well. Oh aye, the parliament will be rocked – but no shattered. Same for your party. They'll survive and they'll need someone to salvage the operation. Someone trusted by the public as a no-nonsense figure, Someone utterly untainted by scandal. One wee email.

ELSPETH: What do you get out of all this?

BEADIE: Money. If the church wants this to happen, they'll have to pay for it.

ELSPETH: Shite Beadie. What's in it for you?

BEADIE: What's in it for me is the same as what's in it for them and for you. Power. Shame is a great motivator Elspeth. And the tabloids know that only too well. We don't want their standards slipping now, do we?

Pause.

BEADIE: You've twenty-four hours.

ELSPETH: I don't need your twenty-four hours. Christ, I don't know why I've even sat listening to you. For all I know you could be bloody taping this conversation. Now that would make sense.

BEADIE: Me making you an offer? It's no a crime to be tempted. Jesus was tempted, remember.

ELSPETH: And in the end he said, 'get thee behind me Satan'.

BEADIE: I thought in the end they nailed him to a tree.

ELSPETH: No Beadie, in the end, he rose again.

BEADIE: But you won't. Not without this.

Scene 6

The CARDINAL's office. SHELLEY and the CARDINAL.

SHELLEY: As I'm sure you appreciate, we are faced with difficult choices.

CARDINAL: Unfortunately, I would say that it is you, and not we, who is faced with a difficult choice. We, after all, did not have this conversation. We, after all, never mentioned forty thousand pound as a fee for Mr Beadie.

SHELLEY: Quite.

CARDINAL: But such considerations aside, it would be you who would have to take this task upon himself, as it's not a decision I feel right or comfortable making for you. I would recommend, therefore, that you take the time to contemplate it over many hours and much prayer, and only after that should you come to a decision. Then, once you have, if you have chosen to act upon Mr Beadie's advice, so be it. If, however, you have not.

SHELLEY: Yes?

CARDINAL: Don't make me answer that. You – Father Shelley – know fine well what you've been up to up there in Redhill Towers on your afternoons aff. It's between you and the Lord. That is all I have to say on the matter Father Shelley. Go now, and God bless you.

Scene 7

BEADIE's house. ELSPETH visits him.

BEADIE: I wasn't expecting you so early. I'm barely out my jim-jams.

ELSPETH: **(handing him the disc)** Forget it.

BEADIE: A wee coffee?

ELSPETH: No thanks. I've got to go.

BEADIE: Ok. But before you do, there's something you should see. You sure about that coffee?

ELSPETH: Just show me what you have to and lets get it over with. What is it today? Planting a bestiality video on Tony Blair?

BEADIE hands her a file. ELSPETH begins reading. It has a profound effect on her and she throws it down.

ELSPETH: What's this? What's this filth?

BEADIE: Transcripts of testimony by former residents of St Saviour's Children's Home, Nettleston. A good few years ago several of these wee kiddies were abused, sexually and physically, by a priest who worked there. Nasty business. Assaulted, raped, sodomised, beaten, a tragically familiar catalogue in these revelatory days, when the past keeps giving away its nasty wee secrets. But the thing is, these nasty wee secrets were given up a long time before now. Oh aye. Of course, there was an inquiry of sorts. And to cut a long and weary story short – well, funnily enough, that's what your father did. Working-class hero, Councillor Joseph Doyle cut a long story short.

ELSPETH: My father?

BEADIE: It was his call to take it to the authorities, but instead he let his beloved church quietly sweep up its own mess. **(Pause.)** It might interest you to know there's a few survivors in the process of suing the Catholic church. Their lawyers know the church covered up what was going on at the home. Right now they don't know who helped. Nor do they have to.

ELSPETH: And you had this last night?

BEADIE: Do you really think I'd hang my balls out there and tell you all about this plan if I couldnae guarantee you'd say yes. What am I, an idiot?

ELSPETH: I've no idea what the hell you are.

BEADIE: Look Elspeth, you needed a helpin' hand to make the right choice. Just take the disc, send the email, reap the reward. And don't stand there all tearful. Doin' it for the sake of your deid father's reputation. Do it for yourself. If you really want to honour the man in his grave, think how honoured he'll be in a few years when his daughter's First Minister.

Act 3

Scene 1

The prison. PARLABANE is about to call SARAH.

SARAH: Hello?

PARLABANE: Hello, Sarah.

SARAH: Jack! Jesus. Thank god its you. I've been going up the wall. I didn't know what to think and you didn't phone and then I was on call and I thought maybe you might have called and not left a message, but then the next night there was nothing and I wasn't sure whether you were safe or whether you'd had some kind of breakdown or been hurt and I couldn't sleep so I wrote to you and then I . . .

PARLABANE: Sarah.

SARAH: Why haven't you called?

PARLABANE: Sarah.

SARAH: Why Jack?

PARLABANE: I've been an arsehole. Will you come and see me? **(To audience.)** His name was Ross Quinn, a third-year specialist registrar, and that rarity in his profession, someone with a conscience. He headed the hospital Trust's junior doctor's committee – and had been working tirelessly in an on-going dispute regarding unpaid overtime. He was a selfless, shrewd, articulate – well-meaning son of a . . .

Scene 2

ROSS grabs SARAH into the store cupboard.

SARAH: What's wrong? Ross – calm down.

ROSS: I . . .

SARAH: You've not told your wife?

ROSS: No.

SARAH: Someone else has told your wife?

ROSS: No.

SARAH: So – what?

ROSS: Sarah, he came out of nowhere.

SARAH: Who did?

ROSS: He'd photographs of us leaving the hotel room, hand-written depositions from hotel staff, an unnamed colleague who could vouch how close we'd been all evening. Christ Sarah, he'd had the bed sheets analysed – condom lubricant, vaginal fluid, the lot. He practically had diagrams.

SARAH: But I don't . . . who'd? . . .

ROSS: The Trust. Who do you think?

SARAH: Bloody hell.

ROSS: I've to back off the campaign, accept the next offer on the table or he takes this to the papers.

SARAH: Why the hell would they want to publish this? Who'd be interested in our wee dirty shag?

ROSS: My wife – to begin with. Sarah, have you read the papers recently? You don't have to be bloody famous, you just have to get caught. Doctors' rights campaigner is love-cheat. Get the picture?

PARLABANE: All of a sudden, following the 4 MSP's in sex-scandal debacle, it was like the early nineties revisited. Naeb'dy wis safe.

Scene 3

SARAH is door-stepped by a reporter.

SARAH: What did you say your name was again?

KEVIN: Kevin. Kevin Simpson.

SARAH: And where are you from Kevin?

KEVIN: The *Daily Recorder*.

SARAH: So how can I help you?

KEVIN: How many times did you cheat on him? How many times did you do it?

SARAH: What?

KEVIN: I hear he's pretty well-endowed. That whit you're used to? We could offer you five hundred quid for your side of the story, a thousand if you pose with your top off. You know we're only gaunny print the story – so you might as well say something.

SARAH: Go back to yir skud mags and yir Clearasil ya wee . . .

BEADIE: **(delighted)** . . . beauty!

Scene 4

Visitor's day in prison. PARLABANE meets SARAH.

SARAH: I'm so sorry Jack.

PARLABANE: I'm the one who flipped my lid.

SARAH: We both did this.

PARLABANE: Wife cheats on you, so you go on some bender and break into the headquarters of the Catholic church. What's that about?

SARAH: You ok?

PARLABANE: Mind and body are still together. To be honest the lobster every night is starting to grind me down a wee bit, but you know, you're not here to enjoy yourself.

SARAH: Jack.

PARLABANE: I'm okay. And I don't mean okay as in I don't want to talk about it. I mean okay as in I'm gaunny get through this. It's a kick in the arse I was big enough to earn for myself, so I'm big enough to take it.

SARAH: We matter Jack.

PARLABANE: It's only a couple of months.

SARAH: And then we can get back to what we had before?

Pause. Neither are entirely sure.

SARAH: Keep your head down and don't do anything stupid.

PARLABANE: I've learned a new respect for the dignity of silence. Anyhow, nobody round here cares aboot a wee scrote like me.

SARAH: I do.

Scene 5

Prison-cell. CHRISTIE and FOOALTIYEMAN.

CHRISTIE: I want that bastard Parlabane taken care of. Thon wee orange cunt – bigoted wee bastard was slaggin' aff the Catholic church in the papers, and noo he thinks he's in the middle a fuckin' Watergate.

FOOALTIYEMAN: Widnae even gie us a fag when ah wis desperate.

CHRISTIE: Same interferin' wee shit that got my brother-in-law a twelve-stretch in Peterheid, an' fucked up oor whole network at the same time.

FOOALTIYEMAN: Your Michael? That wis runnin' the coach trips tae Lourdes an' bringing gear back fae France?

CHRISTIE: Aye. An' it was sweet as a fuckin' nut. Naeb'dy wis gonna search a bus full o' spastics, wir they? Bringin' gallons a pure heroin dissolved in bottles a holy watter, holy pictures dipped in acid. Perfect. The spastics got their wee trip tae Lourdes aw paid fur - and we got the gear. Everyone happy. Then this wee cunt comes along an' blabs it aw tae the paper. **(Giving big hint.)** But ah hear he's gonna be working in the spray painters fae next week.

FOOALTIYEMAN: **(catching on)** Right!

CHRISTIE: This cunt needs tae be taught some respect, an' I'll be generous wi' my gratitude tae whoever administers the lesson.

Scene 6

SHELLEY's office. BEADIE and SHELLEY.

BEADIE: I want that bastard Parlabane taken care of.

SHELLEY: I thought we already had. We gave the papers that story about his wife. What more do we need to do? The guy's a laughing stock.

BEADIE: Do you know what makes this guy tick?

SHELLEY: What's to know? He's a journalist with a bee in his bonnet.

BEADIE: Exactly.

SHELLEY: And there's plenty of those.

BEADIE: Jack Parlabane is the last bloke you want takin' an interest in your affairs – especially Father, given what our affairs have involved in recent times.

SHELLEY: What do you have in mind?

BEADIE: Now we've got him riled up, we need to reel him in. He calls your offices now and again, doesn't he?

SHELLEY: Now and again? He calls all the bloody time. I'm never available.

BEADIE: Well, next time, you will be.

SHELLEY: I will?

BEADIE: Aye – and I'll tell you exactly what you're going to say to him.

Scene 7

SHELLEY and PARLABANE on telephone.

SHELLEY: So, you disagree with our beliefs.

PARLABANE: To put it mildly.

SHELLEY: That's your prerogative. But tell me, what are we supposed to have done so wrong that you're bombarding my office with almost hourly phone calls?

PARLABANE: This 800,000 people.

SHELLEY: Yes?

PARLABANE: That's a fair amount of clout in a democracy, Father. Wouldn't you agree?

SHELLEY: I wouldn't argue with it. Why? Do you want me to?

PARLABANE: And your sources for this are? . . .

Silence.

PARLABANE: Father?

SHELLEY: Our registers of baptisms can be backed up with those educated at catholic schools.

PARLABANE: And once they've left? You can be absolutely sure they still pledge allegiance to the creed and morality promoted on their behalves?

Silence.

PARLABANE: Ok Father – what about last week's congregation statistics?

SHELLEY: These matters are not as simple as how many people might have gone to mass on any given Sunday.

PARLABANE: How many do?

SHELLEY: Faith and belief are deeper matter than attendance figures. This is not Ibrox Park or the Roxy on a Saturday night.

PARLABANE: My point exactly Father. Your flock tend to be a wee bit more on the – shall we say – fallow side.

Beat.

SHELLEY: Of course we keep our own records Mr Parlabane. In fact only last year we carried out a fairly in-depth survey.

PARLABANE: Bet it recorded less than 800,000?

SHELLEY: You'd be surprised.

PARLABANE: Go on – surprise me.

SHELLEY: It was carried out for internal purposes – not for justifying our existence to journalists. In fact, the only place you'd find a copy of it is in this office, and as I said, its purpose was not public, so that's where it's going to stay.

PARLABANE: Hook line and bloody sinker.

Scene 8

PARLABANE stands (as in Prologue) in the middle of a darkened room which could be the Catholic HQ or the spray painters workshop. He holds up the folder SHELLEY has been discussing.

PARLABANE: Gotcha!

FOOALTIɣEMAN appears.

FOOALTIɣEMAN: Gotcha! There's a prize on your heid, and Fooaltiyeman, ahm gonna fuckin' take it.

FOOALTIɣEMAN stabs PARLABANE with a sharpened ruler. PARLABANE falls to the floor holding the folder aloft. SHELLEɣ appears.

SHELLEɣ: Gotcha!

SHELLEɣ grabs the folder. PARLABANE lies in agony on the ground.

SHELLEɣ: A man who finds corruption in every place he looks – might he perhaps be seeing the reflection of what lies within himself?

PARLABANE collapses. He is placed on a hospital trolley. ROSS QUINN appears.

QUINN: Don't worry sir, you're going to be ok. We're going to take you to the hospital. You're going to be taken care of. You're in safe hands now. By the way, I'm Doctor Ross Quinn.

Interval

Act 4

Scene 1

SANDERSON phones BEADIE.

BEADIE: Beadie speaking.

SANDERSON: Hello.

BEADIE: Who's that?

SANDERSON: It's, ehm, David. David Sanderson.

BEADIE: You didn't sound sure for a minute. What can I do for you David?

SANDERSON: Ehm, well, the thing is . . . I've been thinking.

BEADIE: Thinking? I thought you had computers to do that for you.

SANDERSON: The trouble is – their conclusions aren't as reliable as everybody assumes. Not that I need to tell *you* that, Mr Beadie. If you know what I'm getting at.

BEADIE: What do you want, David?

SANDERSON: Like I said, I've been thinking. It's been a dramatic few months in the old politics game, has it not?

BEADIE: To say the least.

SANDERSON: Even I noticed that business with the MSP's and kiddie porn. Quite a story.

BEADIE: Ok – get to your point.

SANDERSON: The point is that you didn't tell me what I was involved with. The point is you gave me no clue what this was really all about.

BEADIE: Oh, bollocks I didn't. I gave you the emails to include in the file for god's sake. All the names were on them.

SANDERSON: But I didn't read them. And as for the server logs, all you gave me was a bunch of usernames. They could have been anybody. If I'd known who they were, Jesus Christ.

BEADIE: Which is why I thought it best for both of us if you didn't.

SANDERSON: I'd a right to know. I'd no idea what I was getting involved in.

BEADIE: Aye, well, its over now, so I don't see what you're getting your knickers in a twist about. Nobody knows what you did.

SANDERSON: You're right. Nobody knows. But it doesn't have to stay that way.

BEADIE: Well, I'm not going to go shooting my mouth off, if that's what you're worried about.

SANDERSON: Actually, its *my* mouth you should be worried about. Those MSP's got six months. Heavy going for a few wee gifs and jpegs. Who'd have known what a storm would blow up out of this? And now, looking at all the facts – it strikes me that five grand was a hellish price for what I provided.

BEADIE: If memory serves David, the price was five grand plus your employers, friends and extended family not finding out about the twelve-year old prostitute in Pattaya.

SANDERSON: She was fourteen, and she looked twice that. I

can say I didnae know. What are you gaunny say, Mr Beadie? Oops, I seem to have slipped and accidentally framed half the fucking government. I could turn queens' witness, I'd cut a deal. You'd be the one who went down.

BEADIE: I'll hang you out to dry, ya cheeky wee bastard. You'll be on the paedophile register in a flash, wi' Mags Hainey an' the angry-mother mob breakin' doon your fuckin' door.

SANDERSON: I don't doubt it. But it doesn't have to come to all that, does it? We can come to an arrangement, cant we?

BEADIE: Cut to the fuckin' car-chase Sanderson. What do you want?

SANDERSON: Fifty grand.

BEADIE: Fif? . . . Get tae . . .

SANDERSON: Per annum.

BEADIE: You're aff yir heid.

SANDERSON: I think, given the scale of what you've pulled off, you should consider this a realistic expense. I mean, lets face it, you didn't do this for a laugh, did you? As long as you keep payin', nobody needs to know how the face of Scottish politics was really changed

BEADIE: I'll change your fuckin' face, you wee prick.

SANDERSON: It's not nice being blackmailed, is it Mr Beadie? Lets see how you like it. You've got a week, or it's gaunny be your mug on the front page for a change.

Scene 2

SHELLEY's office. SHELLEY and BEADIE.

SHELLEY: Thou shalt not kill. One of the ten commandments. Haven't you heard of it?

BEADIE: You got any better ideas, Father? Or have you maybe got a spare fifty large burnin' a hole in your pocket?

SHELLEY: What happened to the forty thousand we gave you?

BEADIE: Who do you think that was for? It was to pay him for his services and his silence. But now the greedy wee shite wants more, so unless you can organise a fast sale of holy relics.

SHELLEY: I can't, I wont countenance such a thing. I don't have the stomach for this one little bit.

BEADIE: Have you the stomach for ten years in jail? That's what we could be lookin' at here. We fucked with the whole democratic process of a parliament people waited three hundred years for – they're no' gaunny let us off with a stern lecture. Just think of everything that's changed in recent months – aw that'll be changed right back – all the things you detest will be totally exonerated. The Catholic church's influence in Scottish society will rank somewhere between Save the Midge campaign and the Geoff Hurst Fan Club.

SHELLEY: I can take the fall for it myself, Mr Beadie. I always knew I might have to. The church will be blameless.

BEADIE: Aye, that will be right. Listen, if I go down, I'm goin' down in flames, an' I'm burnin' everything I touch on the way. There's no' gaunny be any one bad apple malarkey. This went right to the top, and you me and yir precious Cardinal Doollan aw know that.

SHELLEY: But vengeance is mine, says the Lord.

BEADIE: The Lord has options father. You don't. Its time you guys grew your balls back – otherwise you're gaunny end up extinct.

SHELLEY: Our faith has endured sterner tests than this.

BEADIE: Knock the piety on the heid father. You're all a bunch of hypocrites, and I'm gaunny make sure everybody knows it unless you get your act together and get on board.

SHELLEY: I'd rather be a hypocrite than a murderer.

BEADIE: Interesting comparison *Father*. Because going by your precious faith's definitions, you're already baith. Redhill Abortion Clinic. 10am appointment. Bernadette McMenemy.

SHELLEY: You . . . you, fu . . .

BEADIE: Oops. Careful now, Father, your halo's slippin'. You almost said a swearie-word there

SHELLEY: How dare you judge me. You don't know one thing about it – me – my life.

BEADIE: I know enough. I know the parts that matter. I know the parts people will be interested in. Priest. Girlfriend. Love-child. Abortion.

SHELLEY: May God forgive you Beadie, you're an evil evil man.

BEADIE: I don't think you're exactly towerin' above me on the morality ladder here. I don't want to reveal this stuff, but I'm fucked if I'm goin' down because you wouldn't help me.

SHELLEY: Wouldn't help you murder someone?

BEADIE: Oh, get off your high-horse ya pompous prick. Look on the bright side, at least this time it wont be your own flesh and blood.

SHELLEY lunges at BEADIE but is stopped and put in arm-brace.

BEADIE: That's it Father – a wee bit of anger's what we need. Now, try and think how angry you'll feel when everybody knows about Bernadette's wee appointment. Think how angry you'll feel when the pro-choice mob have got all this to play with, on top of everything else. Then think how angry you'll feel when you realise you had the chance to stop it. Do yourself a favour.

As BEADIE is saying the following SHELLEY moves to BEADIE's orders.

BEADIE: There's a hire-car booked in your name. You're collectin' it tomorrow.

SHELLEY is travelling in car.

BEADIE: As you pass Pitlochry, Craggan is signposted fifteen miles north. I'll be driving behind you the whole time – so don't think you can go putting your foot down on that accelerator. When you come to the war monument, turn right, drive about fifty yards, then park at the end of the long, low terrace of houses. If there's anyone about, keep on driving out of town – do a second circuit and when it's all clear, then park. And wait for me. Your part's no' ended in aw this just yet.

The journey comes to an end.

Scene 3

BEADIE and SHELLEY in hotel restaurant.

WAITRESS: Would you like to see the wine list sir?

BEADIE: Nae need. We know exactly what we want.

WAITRESS: What would you like sir?

BEADIE: We would like a bottle of the 1993 Chateau Musar.

WAITRESS: Certainly sir.

BEADIE: And I'll have the pan-fried pigeon breast with crispy leeks and a raspberry vinaigrette.

WAITRESS: **(to SHELLEY)** Sir?

BEADIE: You liked the look of that guinea fowl on a bed of puy lentils, with beetroot and a red wine sauce, didn't you?

WAITRESS: Sir?

SHELLEY: Yes.

The WAITRESS leaves.

SHELLEY: I'll not eat a bite. I don't share your appetites Mr Beadie, for anything.

BEADIE: You know Father, I'd seriously think about cheerin' up and trying to relax if I was you. It's part of your alibi, remember.

The WAITRESS returns with the wine.

WAITRESS: Sir – would you like to taste?

BEADIE: We'll pour our own thanks hen.

The WAITRESS leaves. BEADIE lifts the bottle of wine in one hand, hovers it above his lap, then with his other hand, he picks up an identical bottle from his bag and exchanges the two.

BEADIE: Ribena, Father?

BEADIE pours.

BEADIE: Cheers. **(Tastes.)** Excellent vintage. Look, I'm serious about the cheerin' up business.

SHELLEY: Ur ye?

BEADIE: We don't start looking like were having a rollickin' good time knockin' this stuff back, they're gaunny think we're a pair of alcoholics. Hiv ye no' got a wee joke or something tae lighten the mood?

SHELLEY considers.

SHELLEY: There's these three boy scouts get lost on a camping trip and they come across this old cottage just as night falls. This bloke answers the door. He takes them in out of the rain and is about to serve them some supper when something occurs to him, and he asks them all what religion they are. Two of them say they're Protestants, and the third says he's a Catholic. At this, the bloke tells the wee Prods to go into the living-room, where they sit in front of a roaring fire eating hot soup and sandwiches. The Catholic, meanwhile, has to sit in the cold hall with just stale bread and water. The following morning, when they all wake up, he asks them whether they had any dreams. One of the Prods says he dreamt he was in heaven. What was it like? The host asks. It was just like here – all warm and cosy, with nice food and good company. The other wee Prod says he dreamt the same thing. Then he asks

the Catholic what he dreamt, and he says he dreamt he was
in hell. What was it like? The bloke asks. Well, it was just like
here, the wee fella says. You couldnae get near the fire for
Protestants.

BEADIE laughs.

BEADIE: There's nothing like a wee bit a persecution. But I've
got one for you too. What's the difference between acne and
a Catholic priest?

SHELLEY: I don't know.

BEADIE: Acne waits till you're in your teens before it comes all
over your face.

A PHOTOGRAPHER arrives.

BEADIE: Just in time. Ok Father, get ready for your best pissed-
looking smile.

PHOTOGRAPHER: Excuse me. Can I?

BEADIE: Fire away. Who are you with?

PHOTOGRAPHER: Freelance covering the Highlands and
Perthshire.

BEADIE: So we should make the Sundays?

PHOTOGRAPHER: Aye – smile.

**BEADIE cosies up to SHELLEY and they pose for the picture.
The PHOTOGRAPHER leaves.**

BEADIE: That picture Father, will put both of us more than a
hundred miles away on the night of David Sanderson's

murder. Plus, a dozen witnesses will have watched us drink ourselves silly in the Craggan Moor Hotel restaurant. Are you getting the picture?

SHELLEY: Loud and clear.

As BEADIE says the following they both move into their positions.

BEADIE: When you get back to your room ease your window open quietly. We don't want to go disturbing the other guests. And we'll take the long way round to the other side of the hotel – best to avoid the gravel drive – then cut through the trees and out onto the main road. Then we'll walk to where you parked the hire car. You – Father Shelley – will drive the car to Glasgow.

They are in the car.

BEADIE: Go.

SHELLEY drives.

BEADIE: You know, you drive pretty well, considering how much you drank. Four bottles.

SHELLEY: Tasted pish too.

BEADIE: Thirty quid each.

SHELLEY: Thir . . . that's a hundred and twenty quid for Ribena?

BEADIE: Cheaper than fifty grand Father, that's the way I'm looking at it.

Silence.

SHELLEY: Wait – what if he's not in?

BEADIE calls SANDERSON.

SANDERSON: Hello?

BEADIE: You there?

SANDERSON: Aye, but . . .

BEADIE ends call.

BEADIE: He's there – expecting me with eighteen grand.

SHELLEY: Eighteen? But he's expecting fifty.

BEADIE: Basic psychology. If I said I was gaunny front up with the full whack just like that, he'd be a tube not to get suspicious. Mind you, this guy's an amateur, just a wee wank that doesnae have a clue what he's doin'. Me takin' him so seriously had him creamin' his troosers. He was all yes Mr Beadie, that sounds fine. This one'll do anything for his money. **(Stops.)** Right you. Start saying your Hail Mary's.

Their journey ends. They park outside SANDERSON's. BEADIE puts glove on and buzzes the intercom.

SANDERSON: Hello?

BEADIE: It's me.

SANDERSON: Where the fuck have you been? It's after two.

BEADIE: I know what time it is David. But I didn't fancy walking about Glasgow when the pubs came rollin' oot wi' a briefcase full of money.

SANDERSON: I'll buzz you up.

SHELLEY: **(whispering)** I'm not going up there.

SANDERSON: Who's with you?

BEADIE: That's Father Francis Shelley of the Scottish Catholic church. To whom you should be most polite because he is sponsoring the best part of this transaction.

SANDERSON: Come on up. Only you though.

BEADIE: Not okay. You come down. And bring your car keys.

SANDERSON: Fuck off. Just bring me up the money and get it over with. You're forgettin' who holds the cards here.

BEADIE: And you're forgetting that this is a transaction, not a fuckin' gift. If we get the impression you're just gaunny fuck us around . . .

SANDERSON: I'm not fuckin' anyone around. You're the one that's fuckin' me around. Just bring the fuckin' money up the stairs now.

BEADIE: I'm not prepared to be seen walkin' into your place David. This is all about our wee connection remainin' a secret. I've spent far too long standing here already.

SANDERSON: Who's gaunny see you? It's 2 o'clock in the fuckin' morning.

BEADIE: I don't know. That's the point. And it's a point you should bear in mind too. If our relationship goes public, you wont be gettin' a penny.

Pause.

SANDERSON: All right. I'll come down.

BEADIE: Bring your car keys. And follow us.

SANDERSON: Where are we going?

BEADIE: Just somewhere we can give you the money and you can check it out. Without any pryin' eyes takin' notice.

SANDERSON: Right. Okay.

BEADIE walks to car.

BEADIE: **(to SHELLEY)** He's on his way. **(Waits.)** Well. What are you waiting for?

SHELLEY drives.

SHELLEY: Lets not do this. This is insanity.

BEADIE: You're right – let's not.

SHELLEY: Thank the Lord.

BEADIE: Lets go to jail and let's add conspiracy to murder – because that's what's gaunny happen if we let this fucker go. Get a grip Shelley. I'm no' goin' to jail. Did you no' hear what happened to Jack Parlabane in there? Sharpened steel ruler right through the guts. Now, lets get this done. Take this next left and stop over on the right.

SHELLEY parks.

SHELLEY: For the love of god.

BEADIE leaves the car. He walks over to SANDERSON, shoots him, scatters cocaine, then returns to the car.

BEADIE: Easy prey. Drive!

SHELLEY: God forgive you.

BEADIE: He might, but I know the polis wont'. So get a fuckin' shift on. MOVE!

SHELLEY drives. There is a deep prolonged silence between the two men as they drive through the city and out into the country – only eventually broken by SHELLEY.

SHELLEY: I need to pee.

BEADIE: What?

SHELLEY: I need to pee. Its all that Ribena. I'm bursting.

BEADIE: Oh come on, we're nearly at Pitlochry. You can hold on for another half hour.

SHELLEY: I bloody can't. My back teeth have been floatin' since Cumbernauld. It's been about five hours now.

BEADIE: I don't care. You are not stopping the car. What if the polis pass by and decide to pull over and ask if we need any assistance. First thing they'd do is radio our registration before they even got oot their car.

SHELLEY: We've hardly seen a car since Perth, never mind the polis. I have got to stop. There's a garage in Pitlochry.

BEADIE: Are you mad?

SHELLEY: I'm gaunny piss in my troosers in about thirty seconds. I need to stop.

BEADIE: Christ all bloody mighty. Can you make it another five minutes?

SHELLEY: It'll be close.

BEADIE: There's a picnic stop just after Pitlochry, near Killiecrankie, it's off the road – secluded – there's toilets there. But keep the speed down.

SHELLEY: Give us a break here.

BEADIE: Do you want to go to jail for the sake of thirty seconds?

SHELLEY: At least I'd be able to pee in there.

They arrive at picnic area. SHELLEY rushes out to pee. BEADIE gets out – stretches. All of a sudden, another car drives up.

BEADIE: I don't believe this.

A SALES REP gets out.

REP: Rush hour, eh? This the queue? **(About car.)** I see you're saddled with the same heap of shit as me.

SHELLEY appears.

REP: Tom Heron. Manning Tools. Ring any bells? **(To SHELLEY.)** Hear, I'm sure I know your face. You not with Hewlett-Packard?

SHELLEY: No.

REP: So, who youse with then?

SHELLEY: Canon.

REP: Well, good to see you. Nice to chat with someone for a change – relieves the boredom. Maybe see you here again. Here's my card. You got one?

BEADIE: I've got one. It's in the car.

REP: Hold on – I'm absolutely burstin'.

The REP goes into loo. BEADIE retrieves gun, then follows REP into loo.

REP: Hawd oan a minute – I'm no' into aw that stuff.

The sound of the REP being shot. BEADIE exits.

SHELLEY: Holy Mary, mother of God. What the hell did you do that for?

BEADIE: He'd noted the car, he kent your face, he'd remember bloody plenty if the polis asked.

SHELLEY: And what were they gaunny ask, ya numpty? When there's a murder in Paisley, they don't go on Crimewatch asking if anybody saw anything suspicious in bloomin' Killiecrankie.

BEADIE: Coverin' our tracks.

SHELLEY: We're jiggered. Jiggered beyond salvation. Oh, but wait, we've got mister PR guru here. Maybe you could just sort it all out by puttin' a positive spin on the whole thing.

BEADIE: Actually, maybe I could. But it would have to be a very different kind of murder.

SHELLEY: What?

BEADIE: He said he worked for Manning Tools, didn't he? Keys!

SHELLEY: What are you gaunny do?

BEADIE looks through the REP's pockets.

BEADIE: Good. Condoms. Typical dirty bastard – looking to get his end away while he was far from the wife and weans.

SHELLEY: What do you want with condoms?

BEADIE: Get the guy's jukes off and put one of those on his dick.

SHELLEY: I am not . . .

BEADIE: One on his dick – then one on your finger to stick another one up his arse.

SHELLEY: I am not . . .

BEADIE: Well, would you rather swap for the task of sawin' his heid aff?

SHELLEY: You're surely not gaunny?

BEADIE: Headless corpse in gay horror murder. The papers'll think it's Christmas.

Act 5

Scene 1

PARLABANE in hospital.

PARLABANE: Doctor Ross Quinn, my beloved wife's Christmas shag, had successfully removed part of my colon. Or more accurately, Fooaltiyeman had removed it, and Dr Ross Quinn had merely tidied up afterwards. Not without some turbulence I might add – Dr Ross Quinn swore he could smell faecal matter and reopened to check he hadn't missed another leak. Turns out this was due to the anaesthetist having farted and been too embarrassed to own up. But it's good to know we're all human, isn't it? Lying in a hospital bed with nothing but the Scottish papers to keep me comfort, I'd been dreaming of them putting me under again for a wee bit of light relief. **(Reads.)** Headless punter found at Killiecrankie public loos – Scotland's first gay serial killer. Sounded like gleeful optimism to me. **(Reads.)** Another squalid drug-shooting in Paisley – who gives a toss? **(Scans papers.)** Christ – Ian Beadie with Father Francis Shelley. What's the world coming to I ask you.

A GUARD approaches with PETER LOGAN.

GUARD: Right Parlabane, visitor for you. Logan 47251.

PARLABANE: The Right Dishonourable Peter Logan, ex MP, ex MSP, no doubt regretting that prayer in which he asked god that he be remembered for something other than getting a vibrator stuck up his bum by some ex-page 3 stunna. And sure enough his prayers were answered – he'd be remembered for meddling about with kiddie porn along with three other degenerate MSP's.

GUARD: You've ten minutes Parlabane.

PARLABANE: I see the Scottish prison service have managed to get hold of someone even less popular than me, just to make me feel better. In't that nice?

LOGAN: Very witty Mr Parlabane. What? No vibrator gags?

PARLABANE: No thanks. The insertion of foreign objects into the human body isn't something I find very amusing these days.

LOGAN: I can well imagine. So can the Scottish Prison Service. That's why I've got the permanent escort. My situation makes me somewhat of a stab-magnet.

PARLABANE: Your situation? Public figure or sex-offender?

LOGAN: Thank you for your delicacy.

PARLABANE: Sorry. Is there a cosier New Labour term I should be using.

LOGAN: How about innocent? Stitch-up?

PARLABANE: **(laughing)** Stop it. The surgeon said it could burst my sutures if I laugh too much.

LOGAN: The only naked children I've ever seen pictures of were my niece and nephew when they were about two months old Mr Parlabane. This whole thing was a set-up from beginning to end.

PARLABANE: Come off it Logan.

LOGAN: A porn ring with me, Charles Lenzie, Tommy Gray and Murdo McDonald? Me hang about with the likes of them? Of course it was a set-up.

PARLABANE: Well boo hoo for you. What a dreadful injustice. The best of luck with your campaign. Maybe they'll make a film about you one day – In the Name of the Wankers.

LOGAN: We were convicted principally on the strength of one piece of evidence – a server log.

PARLABANE: Aye aye.

LOGAN: For God's sake, listen!

PARLABANE: Naw – you listen pal. I've no' been in here long, but I've been in long enough, and if there's one thing I've learned, it's that no bugger in this entire place is guilty. Well, I am. I did my crime. And I'm dealing with it. I suggest you try the same.

LOGAN: All I'm saying is whatever's behind this, it must be one hell of a story. Surely as a journalist . . .

PARLABANE: How desperate are you? This really has to be the last throw of the dice. Your spin doctors couldnae save you, your lawyers couldnae clear you, so you're down to this washed-up, disgraced, discredited hack you wouldnae have given the steam aff your shite three months ago – hoping I'll be the rough diamond that turns out to be your salvation. Who'd play me in the film? Al Pacino mibbe?

LOGAN: I came to you because you're getting out on an interim release – that's all.

PARLABANE: Aye – also known as please don't sue the Scottish prison service.

LOGAN: You know, for a journalist, you don't pay much attention to the papers. You might want to read up about the bloke who died. The shooting victim near Paisley.

PARLABANE: What about him?

LOGAN: What did he do for a living?

PARLABANE: Didnae notice. Though it was probably what he did in his spare time that was most pertinent in the end

LOGAN: You reckon? Well, head up pal. Read. His name was David Sanderson, and he was a senior software engineer for Scotia OnLine, internet servers for the Scottish parliament. And while you're at it – ask yourself why Ian Beadie's suddenly all cosy with the Catholic Church. Do your homework Mr Parlabane.

Scene 2

FATHER SHELLEY phones ELSPETH.

ELSPETH: Hello.

SHELLEY: Elspeth?

ELSPETH: Yes?

SHELLEY: It's Fa . . . it's Francis Shelley.

ELSPETH: What's happened?

SHELLEY: Oh, Elspeth. It's a terrible thing we've done. A wicked, wicked thing.

ELSPETH: I know, Father.

SHELLEY: No, you don't. It's so much worse. I . . . Oh God.

ELSPETH: Father?

Silence.

SHELLEY: No. It's too late now. I can't talk. I shouldn't have called. I'm sorry

The call ends.

Scene 3

ELSPETH visits BEADIE.

BEADIE: Nah – nah – don't worry – everything's hunky dory. So Elspeth, things are going fine with the career?

ELSPETH: I'm not exactly setting the heather blazing.

BEADIE: Give it time. You'll find your feet. You just have to lose that rabbit in the headlight look and the world'll be your oyster.

ELSPETH: Maybe I should go see him.

BEADIE: Who?

ELSPETH: Father Shelley. See if he's ok.

BEADIE: He's fine.

ELSPETH: Just a social call.

BEADIE: Very busy man these days. Countin' aw those gate receipts.

ELSPETH: Even still.

BEADIE: Tell you what – why don't I pay him a wee visit? You do what you're supposed tae Justice Minister. Bet you widnae have imagined a year ago I'd be calling you that, did ye?

ELSPETH: No, I . . .

BEADIE: And just remember whit put you there. An' don't you start goin' aw wobbly on me, otherwise I might get a few things off my own chest. If ye see whit ah mean.

Scene 4

PARLABANE is released from prison.

PARLABANE: There wasn't a soul waiting when I got released. I don't know what I was expecting. Some king of fanfare, someone with a megaphone shouting he's oot. Just that strangeness of walking out onto a street with cars and buses passing, and the world so obliviously getting on with itself. Six weeks of containment had been long enough to get used to the idea of the outside being a faraway place. I just thought the journey back to it all would have been longer. But it wasn't. So there I was. Back to everyday reality.

Scene 5

ELSPETH finishes off letter on computer. She tries to send it, but the server is down.

ELSPETH: Damn!

She calls the TECHNICIAN.

TECHNICIAN: Hello, technical support – no this is not a recording – how can I help you?

ELSPETH: Yes, hello, this is Elspeth Doyle, Justice Minister. Sorry to be a bother, but why can't I send my emails?

TECHNICIAN: Cos one of the mains servers is down over at Scotia OnLine in Glasgow. Nothing we can do here. Thank you.

He is about to put phone down.

ELSPETH: Wait. Will it be back up soon?

TECHNICIAN: Who knows? Nobody tells me anything round here.

ELSPETH: I've a very important message to send.

TECHNICIAN: You and the rest of your lot. My phone's not stopped ringing.

ELSPETH: Well, I'm sorry, but isn't there anything you can do? I mean, it's a bit of an inconvenience.

TECHNICIAN: Ah well – so's having yir heid blown aff.

ELSPETH: Sorry?

TECHNICIAN: Senior engineer – killed last week. Prime of life, too!

ELSPETH: Killed? Oh right. Surely not at work?

TECHNICIAN: God, no. Murdered. Gunned down in cold blood oot in Paisley. Dae you lot no' read the papers?

ELSPETH puts the phone down. She then tries to phone SHELLEY.

ELSPETH: Come on, come on. Pick up.

The phone rings out.

PARLABANE: So, Scotland wisnae the Alabama of the north after all. Someone had just wanted us to believe it wis. And this someone had spent a great deal of money, time and energy to ensure we were aw just wan step away fae bad teeth, playing banjoes and shagging our first cousins.

Scene 6

SHELLEY's office. The phone is ringing – but BEADIE enters wearing dog-collar before he can answer it.

BEADIE: Missed yir call there Father.

SHELLEY: What are you doing here? You know I've got this appointment with Parlabane. He's coming here to apologise.

BEADIE: I know. Just thought I'd come to lend you some support.

SHELLEY: What do you mean? I don't need your support. He's the one apologising. And anyway, what do you think you're doing, wearing a dog collar? Are you trying to take the piss?

The telephone buzzer goes.

SHELLEY: Yes Margaret? **(Listens.)** He's arrived?

BEADIE: Tell her to send him up.

SHELLEY: Send him up Margaret.

SHELLEY puts the phone down.

So Beadie, what are you doing here again?

BEADIE stabs SHELLEY through the eye with a steel ruler. He then leaves. On the way out, PARLABANE and BEADIE pass each other in the corridor. As they pass, both men look at each other and then BEADIE walks swiftly away. PARLABANE enters SHELLEY's office.

PARLABANE: Father Shelley?

PARLABANE sees body.

PARLABANE: Fuck!

Before PARLABANE can do anything, the office fills with POLICE OFFICERS.

OFFICER: Stay exactly where you are.

Scene 7

PARLABANE in prison-cell.

PARLABANE: Did I miss the trial? You know, the part where they find out whether I had anything to do with this shit or not? It's just, you seem awfy sure.

The door slams shut.

Act 6

Scene 1

SARAH's house. ELSPETH visits her.

SARAH: Yes?

ELSPETH: My name's Elspeth Doyle.

SARAH: I know who you are. What are you doing here?

ELSPETH: I've some information I need to tell you. Can I come in?

SARAH: Well, if we're talking information – I've some for you too.

ELSPETH: Good – lets see if they tally.

Scene 2

PARLABANE calls SARAH. He's holding a paper in his hands.

PARLABANE: Sarah, I've cracked it.

SARAH: What?

PARLABANE: I know who murdered Shelley.

SARAH: Don't do this to yourself.

PARLABANE: I've the evidence right here in front of me. A picture of Father Shelley having dinner at Craggan Moor Hotel with Ian Beadie.

SARAH: Please stop this.

PARLABANE: Before I found Shelley I passed a priest in the corridor. I thought I recognised the face, but I couldn't put two and two together.

SARAH: Who?

PARLABANE: Ian Beadie. Listen to this **(Reads.)** *Ian Beadie had been working closely with Father Shelley since being hired last year to advise upon the church's dealings with the media. The PR guru says he was shocked and deeply saddened.*

SARAH: Jack, that proves absolutely nothing.

PARLABANE: This guy Sanderson received a call from Perthshire before he died. Beadie and Shelley were slap bang in the middle of deepest Perthshire the night of the murder.

SARAH: But what motive?

PARLABANE: Parliament liberal polices take a dive as church's profile goes through the roof for the first time in years. You do the maths.

Scene 3

SARAH's house. SARAH and ELSPETH.

SARAH: So how long were you going to keep your mouth shut? Who else needed to be murdered? My husband?

ELSPETH: I understand you're upset.

SARAH: My husband is in jail Ms Doyle. He's facing life imprisonment for murdering a priest.

ELSPETH: Then perhaps I can help.

Pause.

SARAH: Well, I'm waiting.

ELSPETH: I was hoping we could help each other.

SARAH: How?

ELSPETH: Jack has a reputation for breaking into places, hasn't he?

SARAH: **(gives her a look)** You taking the piss?

ELSPETH: I mean, there must be something in Beadie's house that ties him to all this. And I was hoping that maybe Jack's passed on some of his secrets to you.

SARAH: Me? Housebreaking? I don't think so somehow.

ELSPETH: Then what? If we don't do something – and quick – we're stuffed.

SARAH thinks.

SARAH: What would you say to a bit of jail breaking?

ELSPETH: What are you thinking?

SARAH: Well, you're Justice Minister. Why have a fancy title if you don't abuse it once in a while?

SARAH: **(laying out plan)** He's spoke of this Mikey Briggs character – who he seems to trust.

Scene 4

PARLABANE and BRIGGS.

PARLABANE: What's this?

BRIGGS: Methylene blue your missus says.

PARLABANE: Don't suppose it could make me disappear?

BRIGGS: Funny you should say that.

SARAH: **(continuing with plan to ELSPETH)** You'll have to contact Beadie.

Scene 5

ELSPETH calls BEADIE.

BEADIE: So, what do you think about all this Parlabane business?

ELSPETH: Prison does strange things to people. Makes them harder, colder.

BEADIE: Careful Elspeth, mustn't let anyone hear the new Labour Justice Minister say a thing like that.

Beat.

ELSPETH: Beadie, I could use some cheerin' up — what with all that horrible business with Father Shelley. I don't suppose you'd be free for a bite of dinner?

BEADIE: When?

ELSPETH: Tomorrow night do?

Scene 6

SARAH: Jack has to then drink the methylene blue.

ELSPETH: And what will that do?

Scene 7

Prison-cell. Two Reliance SECURITY GUARDS on watch over PARLABANE. A scream from PARLABANE. The guards rush over. PARLABANE points to blue pee.

PARLABANE: Guard! Guard!

GUARD 1: Christ almighty. The guy's piss is bright blue.

Scene 8

SARAH: Meanwhile I've a wee favour to ask from Dr Ross Quinn.

Scene 9

Hospital. PARLABANE is wheeled in by two guards. SARAH and ROSS QUINN are waiting.

QUINN: I've theatre ready. There's no time to waste.

GUARD 1 puts handcuff onto PARLABANE.

QUINN: That won't be necessary. This man's in no condition to run away.

GUARD 1: It's staying on.

QUINN: Its going to be very difficult working around his arm if its attached like that.

GUARD 1: The handcuff stays. I'm taking no chances with this wan. Especially if there's scalpels and what-have-you lyin' aboot.

QUINN: He'll be under anaesthetic.

GUARD 1: He murdered a priest this nutter.

GUARD 1 stands resolute.

SARAH: Dr Quinn, this man has orders.

GUARD 1: See – telt ye.

SARAH: But any little disturbance can be life-threatening to the patient when I put him under.

QUINN: Plus the operation will take four hours.

SARAH: I can handle this Dr Quinn.

GUARD 1: Four? You're having me on.

SARAH: And it'll be more comfy out there. You've a telly, magazines, coffee.

GUARD 1: But . . .

QUINN: Where else could he go?

The handcuffs are removed and PARLABANE is wheeled into theatre. They all immediately spring into action. PARLABANE

gets off trolley – SARAH hands him his mobile and keys – ROSS QUINN watches from the side.

SARAH: I've put all your gear in the boot. You've got four hours Jack. If you don't make it back on time, we've all had it.

QUINN: Yes – good luck.

QUINN puts out his hand to shake PARLABANE's. PARLABANE hesitates and then shakes QUINN's hand. SARAH pulls PARLABANE to the side.

SARAH: We can fix it, can't we?

PARLABANE: I'll give it my best shot.

SARAH: I meant us Jack?

PARLABANE leaves.

Scene 10

ELSPETH and BEADIE having dinner at restaurant.

ELSPETH: This is good. I'm starting to feel human again.

BEADIE: You need wee treats now and again to remind yourself why you're knockin' your pan in the rest of the time.

They hold up glasses.

BOTH: Cheers.

ELSPETH: You look like you were in need of a wee bit of *la dolce vita* yourself, if you don't mind me saying.

BEADIE: Hard couple of weeks.

ELSPETH: Hard couple of months.

BEADIE: Tough at the top, eh?

ELSPETH: I've never known pressure like it. But then, it's hardly been the quietest time in the world of politics recently.

BEADIE: Is there ever such a thing?

ELSPETH: All things are relative. But it isn't just the pressures of the job I've had to cope with. The pressures of how I got it haven't been a breeze either.

BEADIE: Sounds like Catholic guilt. Elspeth. There isnae a politician in power anywhere in this world who didnae stab a few backs to get where he wanted. Nature of the game. Regrets and remorse are for memoirs.

ELSPETH: I'm learning that now. I'm also learning to be grateful for the wee shove you gave me. The worst thing wasn't guilt. It was the fear that it would all go belly-up. I was sure the evidence wasn't going to be enough, and if they traced it back, we both knew where the trail would have led.

BEADIE: I don't know what you mean.

ELSPETH: You must be pretty *au fait* with all this new technology. I mean, being able to organise all that stuff with the email. How you did it I'll never know.

Pause.

BEADIE: Elspeth, mind if I ask you something?

ELSPETH: Fire away.

He reaches down and retrieves the Dictaphone from her person.

BEADIE: **(into Dictaphone)** Do you think my heid buttons up the back? Don't try an' play games with me. I wrote the fuckin' book.

He drops the Dictaphone on her plate, splashing her front.

BEADIE: Dinner's on you.

BEADIE leaves.

Scene 11

PARLABANE is dangling from BEADIE's ceiling.

PARLABANE: The trick is to leave no evidence. Any little trace of a detail, any wee slip, can come rushing straight back at you.

PARLABANE's phone goes off as he is dangling mid-air. He somehow manages to answer.

PARLABANE: Hello.

ELSPETH: Jack.

PARLABANE: Jack's kinda busy at the moment, can I take a message?

ELSPETH: Its Elspeth Doyle. He's on his way home. Have you found anything yet?

PARLABANE: I'm only just inside. Where did you go for dinner? McDonald's?

ELSPETH: He walked out. He rumbled me.

PARLABANE: How long have I got?

ELSPETH: Twenty minutes. Twenty-five at most. You might have to turn back.

PARLABANE: I love pressure. I live for pressure.

ELSPETH: What?

PARLABANE: Too late now.

He slides down to the floor.

ELSPETH: Be careful.

PARLABANE is now in a room full of laser beams he has to carefully pass through without touching.

PARLABANE: I'd never seen anything like it. So neat. A testament to Beadie's meticulous nature. Folders everywhere. He had to have a record of just about every petty indiscretion, every unfortunate act of human weakness committed by anyone in Scotland who met the minimum public profile or income-bracket criteria. Call Guinness – I've located the world's saddest wank. There was only one thing I was looking for. Beadie's gun. If Beadie's prints were on it, that was all I'd need. Ballistics would match it to the bullet that killed Sanderson. The cops would then start to listen. Beadie's clever alibi would tie Shelley to the Sanderson shooting, providing a motive for him to then kill the priest, and after that, they'd search Beadie's house and find the folders and the computer. If Beadie's prints are on the gun.

PARLABANE opens the gun-case and takes out a Sternmeyer P-35 11 mm pistol. He holds it up in preparation for BEADIE walking in. Eventually, BEADIE does so.

PARLABANE: Welcome home Beadie.

BEADIE: Oh my God oh Jesus Christ oh fuckin' Jesus God.

PARLABANE: I didn't realise you were so religious Beadie. Must have been all that hangin' about with Father Francis Shelley.

BEADIE: But you're . . .

PARLABANE: In jail? Day release.

BEADIE: I'm warning you Parlabane. You fuck with me and there'll be hell to pay.

PARLABANE: That's ok with me. I know the boss. Now, I'm sure I don't need to tell you how much damage these things can do to the human head. On your knees.

BEADIE kneels.

PARLABANE: I wont mess about playin' games like Elspeth did. I'll just tell you the deal. We both know the situation I'm in, and we both know how that situation came about. So the way I see it, if I just stick this gun up a wee bit closer, like say, to here, and blow your brains all over the wall, then all I'd have to do would be to stick the gun in your right hand **(Makes him touch gun.)** and my problems would be solved. How I'd love to do it. Nothing would give me more pleasure. And there'd be no trace back to me.

BEADIE: You don't seem to understand. It disnae have to be like this. We could come to some kind of arrangement.

PARLABANE: Naw Beadie, you don't seem to understand. I'm under general anaesthetic right now, fifty miles away, to which I have several witnesses, two of them prison officers. I've left no negligible damage, no prints — unlike your good self.

PARLABANE picks up the telephone and dials his home number.

You're calling me at home – just so's you know. Don't worry – I'll leave 10p on the table when I leave. State your name for the benefit of the tape.

BEADIE: You . . .

PARLABANE: Now now. Name.

Long pause as BEADIE considers whether to speak. PARLABANE holds the gun tighter to his head.

BEADIE: Ian.

PARLABANE: Ian what?

BEADIE: **(eventually)** Beadie.

PARLABANE: The questions are going to get a teensy bit harder. And please bear in mind that this confession is for your benefit. I already know the answers, so if you tell any porkies – bang!

BEADIE breaks down in chair. His scream goes on for a while.

Epilogue

ELSPETH's office. PARLABANE and ELSPETH.

PARLABANE: So it's true, you're resigning?

ELSPETH: The parliament doesn't need people like me.

PARLABANE: I'll not argue with that.

ELSPETH: And when Beadie's trial begins, we'll see. **(Beat.)** You get under peoples skin Jack. You ask questions. You see the ugly truths of life manipulating and beating the system every day of life. What keeps you going?

PARLABANE: I . . .

ELSPETH: And no jokes please.

PARLABANE: I don't want to end up like them – or you.

ELSPETH: So you're setting an example? Is that it?

Silence. Beat.

ELSPETH: Well, that's me almost cleared for the next person to step into my shoes.

PARLABANE: **(beat)** Look Elspeth, I came here today because I've something to give you.

ELSPETH: A wee going away card? How awfully kind. Naeb'dy else has bothered.

PARLABANE: **(holding up folder)** This was lying on Beadie's desk. I nabbed it before the police arrived.

ELSPETH is cautious about taking it.

PARLABANE: Don't worry. Nobody knows.

ELSPETH takes the folder.

ELSPETH: I don't know whether to say thank you or not.

PARLABANE: I guess it's what he used.

ELSPETH: So you've read it? Well, my father was many things. And if colluding with the Catholic church to protect its priests, was one of them, then so be it. The truth will out.

PARLABANE: Elspeth – I think you should read it.

ELSPETH: I've no taste for it I'm afraid.

PARLABANE: Tell me – what did Beadie do? Flash it in front of your face?

ELSPETH: I read enough.

PARLABANE: I don't think you did. What did he do Elspeth? Tell you a story then let your fears do the rest?

ELSPETH: I don't understand.

PARLABANE: Elspeth – this file doesn't mention your father's name once. I'm sorry.

PARLABANE puts down the file. He then leaves the office, leaving ELSPETH with the file.

The End